Professional Grief and Bereavement Course

The KEW Training Academy

Professional Grief and Bereavement Course

Copyright

Table of Contents

Contents

Introduction

Welcome to this specialised course on grief and bereavement counselling. This is an add-on course to any counselling qualification enabling you to specialise in an emotive area of life. Each and every one of us will experience the pain of grief and will endure the process of bereavement at some time in our lives. As part of the human condition, it's an expected, even anticipated and yet unwelcome intrusion where no one is prepared fully for the moment of loss. This is why grief and bereavement counsellors are so important as they can use the relevant techniques and understanding to help their clients move forward beyond the pain of loss and take steps towards healing recovery.

This course is intense and is written with qualified counsellors in mind as it does not provide all of the techniques of general counselling. It is possible to study this course alongside a general counselling course if you wish to qualify in this field of expertise at the same time.

Divided into modules, each section details an aspect of the grief and bereavement process so that you can understand and identify with the stages of emotional pain and connect and support your clients as they begin to heal.

Grief and bereavement counselling is not easy. It takes a great deal of patience and understanding of the human condition and an integral need to help those who are at the lowest point of their lives. Although grief is natural, it brings a complicated set of emotions. Depending on the clients' background, relationship with the deceased and their personal experiences in life, the grieving process may not run its natural course and this is when a counsellor can help to free them from stagnating within the most volatile of emotions – anger, avoidance, regret or even relief.

Please take your time when working through this course ensuring that you understand each module before progressing. Your ability to help others depends upon your comprehension of the stages of grief and knowing how to lead your clients towards a healthier state of mind so they can move on with their lives productively.

At the end of each module you will find self-help assessments and we suggest you complete each one before moving onto the next module as it will help you to reflect and consider fully and will consolidate the learning process.

At the end of the course, you will find a final test paper which must be completed alongside some role-play case studies and sent to The KEW Training Academy for review. If completed to a satisfactory level, a professional qualification can be awarded.

If you are ready to proceed, turn to Module One.

Module One

Attachment, Loss and Grief

The human condition is complex. When it comes to death or the loss of someone close, people grieve in very different ways. It may be a natural event and yet it is one that we are so unprepared for in life. We are aware of the existence of death and the futility of avoiding it on a personal level but we often fear it and are unprepared as to the enormity of it and the associated emotions.

Although grieving is a long process in the main, there are correct ways in which to grieve so that the experience leads towards a healing conclusion.

The prospect of loss is considerable and it can affect every aspect of an individual's life and there are considerable wide-ranging emotions experienced as a result - from anger to intense sadness to denial and disbelief. As you can imagine, it can be difficult to help your clients through these extremes of emotions and back toward normality but it is satisfying as you do so.

To be able to understand fully the devastating impact of loss, it is important to have a deep understanding of the meaning of attachment. As human beings, we create strong bonds with others and it can seem impossible to imagine how the strength of any connection can be broken even through death. Denial or avoidance are common emotions when death has occurred suddenly and without warning.

Research into the grieving process is ongoing but it indicates that people develop bonds with others because of specific biological needs i.e. food, sex, security and safety. While these needs develop throughout life, some develop very early on and endure. Attachment behaviours are powerful and remain present.

With this in mind, it's little wonder that when someone dies and we are strongly attached to this person, the response is both deep and intense. The greater the potential for loss, the resulting actions will be varied and emotions, more intense. Although, each and every one of us face loss in life, we all grieve differently.

To understand the real impacts of loss, you must understand the meaning of attachment. There is much research and published work in both psychiatric and psychological literature referring to attachments and how they develop. The late British psychiatrist John Bowlby devoted much of his time to the study of attachment and loss and wrote prolifically upon it. He studied ethology, cognitive psychology, neurophysiology as well as developmental biology in his effort to understand attachment.

He refuted the theory that attachment between people develops just to have biological needs met. He did agree that attachments came from an individual's need for safety and security and this develops very early on but is usually focused towards a few individuals. These attachments are enduring but is normal behaviour. This however was different from the aforementioned feeding and sexual behaviour. His theory is supported by the developmental process that when a child starts to explore the world, extending the nearby boundaries leaving the figure of attachment for longer periods of time but would always return for support or for safety reasons.

Therefore, if something happens to the attachment figure, the response would be one of great anxiety. He suggests that parents therefore provide the security (the foundations) from which the child is able to explore.

George L. Engel, an American psychiatrist felt that when the figure of attachment is lost, it is as psychologically traumatic as being severely wounded is physiologically traumatic. So grief represents a departure from health and well-being and therefore, just as healing would be necessary physiologically, a period of time would be needed to return the individual to a normal state of psychological balance. He felt that the process of mourning should be compared to the process of healing. Certainly healing can be restored in time but equally, sometimes there is inadequate healing and impaired function.

Normal or acute grief

- Bodily distress
- Guilt
- Hostile reactions
- An inability to function
- Preoccupation with the image of the deceased
- Developing character traits belonging to the deceased

Typically, intense feelings of sadness will be one of the most common feelings experienced by those who have experienced the loss of someone close to them. Although some people in the midst of the grieving process find it impossible to cry, this is generally a stage in which they are unable to accept the situation and may even feel numb. Crying is associated with feelings of sadness and is a visible sign of their inner bleakness but some people try to block these feelings, keeping themselves busy. It is only when all the activity stops that when alone, sadness can be overwhelming.

Anger is also a common emotion.

Within your counselling role, anger is not unexpected. It occurs often because the individual is angry at their loved one for dying and leaving them. Their levels of anger may be linked to the level of love felt and can lead onto other volatile emotions. Anger may not even be fully acknowledged. Certainly feelings of confusion and anger lie at the root of many grieving problems and can become a part of a more complex mourning process. Sometimes anger originates as a sense of frustration perhaps during those times when there was nothing that could be done to prevent the outcome.

When someone close to you dies, there may be a tendency to regress. Certainly we experience feelings of helplessness and wonder at the meaning of life without this individual. This leads onto doubts about being able to cope or even if survival is possible without them. Along with confusion, disbelief is often present. When you see clients who seem angry or talk about being angry, this can be a mask that hides their inner fears even without their being aware. Anger can also be a sign of displacement or it can be directed towards another person. It is not uncommon for your clients to express anger towards family members, friends, God, the doctor. Sometimes your clients will turn their anger inwards. This can lead to severe depression or even suicidal behaviour.

Guilt and self-reproach

When someone important has died, it's all too easy to feel a sense of guilt and then self-reproach if an individual feels they didn't do enough, or perhaps had not been kind especially towards the end. These are common feelings and is often experienced by those who have survived. If a death has been traumatic, you may find that those who were present at the time also feel guilt just because they survived and their loved one didn't. Usually, this guilt is irrational but sometimes the guilt can be real and deserved and this makes the situation much harder within counselling sessions.

Anxieties

Some clients may demonstrate severe anxieties. This can quickly lead towards panic attacks. The more intense and persistent the attack, can indicate an abnormal grief reaction. Anxieties often occur because the individual is worried that they cannot cope without their loved one. This can happen at any stage of someone's life but it's easy to see how difficult it could be for a wife or husband to cope without their marital partner after 50 years of togetherness. Equally, if a young man or woman is left to cope after their loved one has died, it can be difficult for them to even conceive how to cope especially if they have children. Irrespective of their actual circumstances, anxiety and panic attacks can occur through internalising worries and struggling to come to terms with all that has happened. This is quite common. Anxiety can also occur through their heightened sense of mortality, if unresolved, this can also develop into a phobia.

Loneliness

Feeling intense loneliness is common after a loss. There is an almost impossible void to fill and it can take time for this to pass. The effects of loneliness can be far-reaching and this emotion can be present even if the individual is surrounded by family and friends.

Fatigue

Clients will often state that they feel exhausted and will be experiencing intense fatigue. It may be apathy or even listlessness but the feelings are overwhelming in its intensity. Fatigue is also self-limiting in that it affects the ability to recover but it can also be indicative of clinical depression.

Helplessness

Feeling helpless is an integral part of the grieving process as is feeling frustrated over the loss. There is no control as to the outcome and it can be hard to accept the inevitable.

Shock

Whether death is expected or not, it can still generate feelings of stress and shock. When death is traumatic, unexpected or sudden, shock can be instant and overwhelming.

Pining

Pining is a very common feeling in connection with loss. It is very strong at the start when the loss is at its most vivid and the individual has to absorb the reality of their situation. When it starts to diminish, it is indicative that the individual has started healing. If the feelings do not stop, it can indicate that traumatic grief is present.

Relief

Some clients will admit to feeling relieved after their loved one has died. This is quite a common emotion experienced after someone has endured a long and painful illness. Strong feelings of guilt are often associated with relief.

Numbness

Numbness is an emotion experienced very early on in the grieving process. It often occurs because there are so many feelings to deal with at that moment of notification that the individual becomes overwhelmed and they are not able to process everything. When numbness sets in, it occurs as a protection, there is no evidence to suggest that it is an unhealthy response.

Varying signs of the grieving process will be present during a counselling session but it is important to note where feelings exist for abnormally long periods of time and when intensity results in complicated reactions to grief.

There are also physical sensations to consider and these are often reported by clients who are experiencing not just emotional loss but physical symptoms too:

- Tightness in the chest and throat
- Feeling sensitive to noise
- Feeling hollow or empty in the stomach area
- Feeling short of breath
- Having a lack of energy
- Weakness in the muscles

- Depersonalisation-when nothing seems real
- Dry mouth

As we are all unique individuals, it is understandable to think that we deal with grief differently. In fact, we seem to face it instinctively but are also, driven by our ability to deal with painful experiences. The amount of support will make a difference too.

We are likely to experience a multitude of thought patterns relative to the whole experience of grief but it is worth noting that sometimes thoughts can become unhealthy and lead towards depression or anxiety.

Some clients will admit that they cannot believe what has happened and it feels as if they are trapped in the midst of a nightmare. Those newly bereaved will often specify that their thought patterns are confused and jumbled and they are unable to concentrate or, have become increasingly forgetful. We can also become preoccupied with thoughts about the deceased and this leads towards obsessiveness. Sometimes clients will admit thinking repetitively about how badly they feel as if they are the victim. Their focus is turned inwards. They may also feel guilt.

Presence

You may find that clients will continue to talk to their loved ones as if they are still there. Although they may be worried by this behaviour, it is actually quite common. Certainly the first few weeks after death, there is often a strong feeling of a presence. Some clients will find it comforting, others will not. Some clients will experience hallucinations both visually and auditory and this is also not unusual. It often occurs within a few weeks following their loss and this generally does not equate to a more complicated mourning experience. While some will find it disconcerting, others may actually find the experience helpful. It's important to not speculate whether the solution is a real or not. From a counselling perspective, it is more important that the client is able to talk to you about it.

Understandably, some behaviours will be affected as a result of feelings of grief. Certainly appetite can be impacted as well sleep patterns altered. The client may have less social interaction too and act in an introverted manner. Absentmindedness is also common. These behaviours usually correct themselves.

Sleep

Sleep disturbances are very common in those who are experiencing the early stages of grief. Although sometimes they will require medical assistance, usually, sleep patterns return to normal in time. If a client has little sleep, it may be worth advising them to seek medical assistance. If a sleep disorder is created as a result and continues, there may be an underlying depressive disorder and this should be explored. It is worth noting that sleep disorders sometimes symbolise fear and this may include the fear of dreaming or the fear of mortality or not being able to wake up. Sometimes, there is a fear of being in the bed alone.

Dreams

It is certainly very common for someone in the process of grieving to dream of the person who has died and it is often a dream where the loved one is still alive but may evolve into dreams that are highly distressing or even nightmares. While the dreams serve a number of purposes, and may give some clue as to the progress of mourning, often clients will need reassurance. By understanding the type of dream experience, it is possible to help apply therapy techniques so to bring these issues to the fore. This can be the catalyst required to start the full healing recovery process.

Avoidance

You will find that some clients do everything possible to avoid talking about the deceased or, doing anything to trigger any painful memories of their grief. This can mean avoiding the place where the person died, or even getting rid of objects that remind them of the person they have lost. The strength of these reactions can be anything from putting away photos to considering moving away i.e. selling the house or changing jobs. When someone gets rid of everything associated with the deceased person very quickly, this can lead towards a complicated grief reaction as it is not healthy behaviour.

It is not uncommon for clients to specify that they regularly call out the name of their loved one hoping to see or hear some sign of their presence. While some are vocal, others will think the person's name sending out longing thoughts for a visitation. It can certainly continue for some time inwardly.

You will also see those clients who seem to sigh frequently and this may be as a result of their oxygen and carbon dioxide levels being similar to those with severe depression.

Crying

We have often considered tears to be part of the healing process and certainly, because stress and trauma serves to cause a chemical imbalance within the body, there is a line of thought that tears will help to remove any toxic substances. Certainly tears will relieve some emotional stresses but research continues.

Grief and depression grief may appear similar to severe depression. Certainly, one can lead towards the other and your client may exhibit depressive symptoms, but the main difference is that the client's self-esteem will not be impacted as a result of grief where it is in clinical depression.

Module One

Self-Study Assessments

Task:

List the physical symptoms that may be experienced by clients

Task:

Explain why feelings of guilt may be natural after loss

Task:

What do we mean by avoidance?

Please note that these self-assessment tasks are to ensure your understanding of the information within each module. As such, do not submit them for review with KEW Training Academy.

Module Two

The Mourning Process

It can be useful to look at the mourning process by way of stages. Those who have studied grief often list up to nine stages of mourning although others will indicate that there are twelve stages. Counselling sessions should be open and honest so it pays to discuss these stages with clients although the journey is very much on an individual level. While it can be hard to define a stage to a client, they should know that people do not always follow the stages to the letter and some people seem to skip a stage.

There are four phases of mourning:

1: Feeling numb
2. Pining
3. Despair or disorganisation
4. Reorganising behaviours

Ultimately, grieving takes time and there are tasks which they can do to help aid the grieving process.

Task One: Accept the reality

When death is sudden, there will always be a feeling that it can't be real. Therefore, the very first step of the grieving process is the hard reality that the individual is really dead and has gone and, will not be returning. This first step is very hard for people and takes time.

Some people will experience denial and refuse to believe that the death is real. There is a tendency to become deeply embroiled in the grieving process. They may even continue as usual right down to setting a place for the deceased at the dinner table. They may also protect themselves from the reality of their situation by denying the actual meaning of the loss i.e. 'I don't miss him/her at all' or, 'he wasn't a good father' etc.

Others remove all reminders of the individual so as to minimise their loss. This is still avoidance even if through action.

Task Two: Process the pain

It is important that the individual acknowledges the reality and begins to work through the pain experienced. This is not just emotional pain but the manifestation of any physical symptoms. Of course not everyone will experience the same intensity of pain but few experience a loss without some sort of emotional angst. Those that specify they felt little after death may be individuals who find it difficult to become attached to anyone. Some people short-circuit this step by cutting off their feelings, thereby denying pain.

Some clients will hinder their own process of recovery by avoiding any painful thoughts. Instead, they may turn to idolising their loved one or the opposite, avoiding all reminders. In fact, alcohol and drugs are often ways in which people stop themselves from progressing through the second task. You may even find some clients who are unable to settle thereafter and who start to travel on a geographic basis in a way to find themselves rather than allowing themselves to process the pain. It is an important part of grief counselling to ease clients through this difficult second task so that they do not carry the pain with them continuously throughout the rest of their lives. Indeed, if they are unable to process task two, additional therapy is likely later on and it may be much harder to go back and work through the pain second time around.

Task Three: Adjustment

There are three areas of adjustment required after death. The individual has to adapt to a new type of environment without their loved one and it can take quite a long time for someone who has lost a partner to realise that they can continue alone. Indeed, it can take months after the loss. There are also the physical practicalities too – living alone, empty house syndrome, managing finances, raising children etc.

In fact, often a client may specify that they didn't realise how important their loved one was to them until now. Those left behind have to develop new skills and take on additional roles as part of the recovery process.

Internal adjustments: Death can affect an individual on so many levels. The person left behind has to consider who they are and how they continue. Some (women in particular) may have to re-establish or discovery their identity afterwards as they may have wrapped their whole life around this individual. So bereavement is muddied by the loss of the person but also without having a sense of their own identity or strengths.

Grieving can also affect a person's self-efficacy so they feel less control over their lives as a result. They may feel helpless or inadequate and certainly vulnerable. They need to ask themselves questions i.e. who am I? How am I different now?

Spiritual

Death can certainly shake the foundations of an individual's belief. In fact, the fundamental values of life and even philosophical beliefs are likely to be challenged. You may hear a client specify that they have lost all direction in life and are now searching for the meaning of this loss in a way just to make sense of it all. This often happens where there is a sudden or untimely death.

Task Four: Finding and enduring

The fourth task is difficult because it takes time before an individual can be fully healed ready to move on with their lives. Although it's a long process towards full recovery, this next part of the healing journey is relevant. You'll note when the client is almost at this stage or when they've already entered it. It's good to support them through these healthy changes but note that they may still experience feelings of guilt or even self-loathing. They are not out of the woods in terms of recovery yet.

Your task is to help them to forge strong new relationships while keeping a place in their hearts for those they have lost. Without our assistance, they will fail to live fully. This happens when the client holds onto past attachments. It prevents them from forming new attachments and because the pain of loss is so intense, it may put them off trying again. Many of your clients are likely to stop at this point. If a client is not ready for this step, re-visit the former task or any area of development that is needed. Grieving is an individual and fluid process. You must act instinctively so to help your clients.

Understanding the mediators

As a counsellor, it is important that you understand the second part of the whole mourning process which is known as the mediators of mourning. By studying grief and its effects on people, you will note a wide range of behaviours all with individual differences. After all, grief can be an incredibly intense experience or it can be a mild one. Some people start the grieving process the moment they hear about the loss while for others, mourning is delayed. So from a professional perspective, you must understand that people cope with mourning in a variety of ways.

1. Find out more about the deceased. If you really want to understand how to help your client, understand more about them and their relationship with the person who has died.
2. In addition to finding out more about the deceased individual, you also need to understand the attachment that the client has to the deceased. It makes sense to discover the strength of this attachment and also, the security factors of the attachment.
3. The extent of positive vs. negative feelings about the relationship i.e. Does the client feel that he or she did enough?
4. The conflict history between the client and the deceased. This is not just about the time of death but any earlier conflicts too. This also relates to unfinished business and long standing conflicts which may lead to guilt.
5. Dependent relationships. If the client was dependent on the deceased, the transitional period of adaptation can be harder and take longer.

The cause of death – this is an important part of the client/counsellor process because by understanding how an individual died, it affords an insight into how the client might truly feel. Use the NASH categories listed below:

- Natural,
- Accidental
- Suicidal
- Homicidal

Consider where the death occurred. Was it locally or miles away? Where was the client at the time? Consider that when the death happens far away, it also makes it far more difficult to believe. If the death was sudden, this can also lead to the situation feeling unreal.

Violent or Traumatic Deaths

The effect of a violent or traumatic death on any survivor is long-lasting. In addition, it will often lead onto complicated mourning. It challenges survivors i.e. those closest to the deceased as to how they can adjust internally and externally and cope with life afterwards, let alone start to lead healthy productive lives once more. It can shatter the individual's view of the world and lead them towards highly volatile emotions.

Multiple deaths

You may see clients who have lost not just one loved one but who has experienced multiple deaths in a short period of time. There can often be grief overload at this time – and the client is likely to struggle to manage their feelings.

Preventable deaths

If a death is perceived as preventable, there is likely to be strong feelings of guilt or blame as a result. These feelings must be worked through to avoid any prolonged period of mourning or complicated grieving.

Ambiguous deaths

On occasion, you may see a client who is not certain if their loved ones are dead. They may be missing and this doesn't truly allow the client to grieve and yet makes it very difficult to remain strong and hold onto feelings of hope.

Suicide or stigmatized deaths

If a loved one has died from a disease such as Aids or has taken their own life, there is often a feeling of not being able to discuss their death openly or to be able to mourn properly. There is a stigma to these types of deaths whereby the individual will often receive less support.

History

When you counsel a client, much of the process is about listening and drawing their emotions out so they can be expressed and discussed. You must also prompt to know more about the deceased person and, more about the client too. If the client has experience many losses, their mental health also needs to be considered. They may have experienced severe depressive bouts and even have unresolved grief and issues to contend with.

Coping

Each individual will have their own coping style – depending on their experiences, feelings, ability to handle anxiety and stress. There are three main coping functions

- Problem-solving
- Active emotional coping
- Avoidant emotional coping

In addition to the above, it's worth considering the client's attachment style by probing into the client's background as these are set up early in life – through the bonding of parent and child. These attachment styles are often seen as traits which are pliable under stress and traumas. If the attachment figure dies, there are determining factors as to the client's ability to grieve normally i.e. how secure might they feel?

The client may feel an overwhelming need to remain close to the attachment figure even though death has severed the link. They try to find a way to rekindle that lost relationship. Eventually, the client understands the permanence of death. A healthy solution for grieving is when the client internalises the deceased so that there is psychological proximity and this means that they no longer seek physical proximity. The love and memory remains, yet, they accept the loss.

Some clients will demonstrate a secure attachment style and will have positive mental models in that they feel valued and worthy. These individuals will still feel the pain of loss but are able to process it and progress while retaining bonds with anyone they have lost.

Insecure attachment styles

There are four types of insecure attachment styles:

1. Anxious/preoccupied
2. Anxious/ambivalent
3. Avoidant/dismissing
4. Avoidant/fearful

Anxious/Preoccupied Attachment

These are the type of relationships that cause uneasiness. The individual is often very sensitive. They may not feel good about themselves and their self-esteem levels may be determined by the focus on others. They often have high levels of stress or chronic and prolonged grief. They may not be able to handle stressful situations well. They may tap into avoidance behaviours. They are often clinging. To help someone in this category, it's important to guide them toward aiming for internalising psychological proximity rather than physical proximity.

Anxious/Ambivalent Attachment

Love and hate will exist almost evenly. They see others as being less than dependable. Their relationships and connections with others may be more than a little volatile. If death is experienced, there is an intensity of anger and anxiousness – this will be excessive. They tend to talk about their former loved ones with reverence making them larger than life. When listening to the client, you may wonder if it is possible for anyone to be this great.

Acknowledgment as to the range of emotions is important, anger must be expressed.

Avoidant/Dismissing Attachment

An individual may have had an unresponsive parent and these experiences could lead toward a self-sufficient lifestyle even if this acts as an emotional shield. As such, behaviours are very much focused on being independent and feeling reluctant to rely on others. Even after death, these individuals may have less emotional reactions because there were less attachments. To clarify, these clients may have a negative opinion of others and so even when faced with periods of great stress, they will not willingly turn to others.

Avoidant/Fearful Attachment

These individuals find it more difficult to come to terms with loss and adapting is equally problematic. They form what is known as tentative attachments created largely through the fear that the attachments may become broken. They are highly susceptible to developing depression. In many ways, a depressed state might form a degree of protection against any inner anger experienced but in the main, you will see these clients also withdrawing on a social level. Withdrawal also leads to protection of self. If you consider that healthy attachments lead the individual toward natural grieving, those less than healthy attachments lead toward anger and guilt once attachments have been broken.

When is mourning finished?

This is a question you may be asked this by clients who are desperate to stop feeling the intensity of emotional and physical pain, but there is no quick and easy answer. Mourning may take months or even years. Once they are able to think about the deceased without experiencing pain, this is a good measure that the mourning period has passed. There may still be feelings of sadness but one that lacks the terrible impact of before.

Module Two

Self-Assessment Tasks

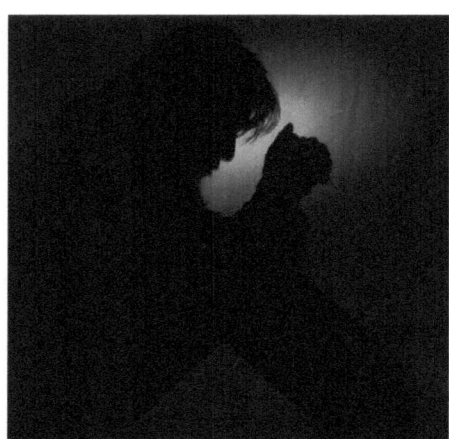

Task:

Consider your own grief experienced (if any) or if not, the grief experienced by someone close to you. How did they/you move through the grieving process?

Task:

Explain in-depth the first stage of the mourning process.

Please note that these self-assessment tasks are to ensure your understanding of the information within each module. As such, do not submit them for review with KEW Training Academy.

Module Three

Grief Counselling

In counselling terms, clients who have experienced a loss of someone close to them are likely to endure a broad range of grief reactions and in the main, people are able to work through this period of mourning on their own. They may have to make little adaptations to make the loss bearable but they will not necessarily need the same level of counselling (if any). But you will see some clients who are experiencing high levels of distress and who believe that they cannot go on without their loved one. Depending on their progression within the grieving process, it is likely that this person is at risk for a poor grief outcome.

As a councillor, your role is to help your clients work through their time of mourning within a reasonable timeframe. Although grieving is a natural process, for some people counselling is more than needed, it is essential.

The type of counselling required will depend on the individual, the relationship that they had with their loved one and how able they are to adapt and even accept this death. Certainly, many people will struggle with the intensity of their thoughts and feelings and their behaviours will be impacted as a result. The ones who seek out your services are the lucky ones in some ways because they are at least aware that they need help. Equally, there may be others who definitely need help but do not seek out counselling and these are likely to extend their grieving process.

Goals

When you take on a client for the first time, the overall goal must be to help this individual adapt to the loss of their loved one. This means, helping them to be accept their situation even though it is likely to be painful.

So we need to look at specific goals as regards the four stages of mourning:

1. It is important to increase the reality of the loss
2. To aid the client to cope with both emotional pain and behavioural pain
3. To aid the client to overcome obstacles and to readjust
4. To enable the client to reinvest in life but still maintain the connection with the deceased

Starting the process

Grief counselling usually begins about a week or so after the funeral. Even when there is a distinct need, the client has to deal with the organisational needs of the time, whether they are in shock or not. They may not even be ready to come to terms with their confusion as often, the brain has a way of adapting and switching off i.e. when feeling numb. If you have been involved in the family's lives leading up to the deaths i.e. perhaps the death was expected, apart from offering condolences, it is still best to delay counselling for a week or more following the funeral service although there is no hard and fast rule on this.

It depends on the clients, the death and the role that has been defined.

If you are already a counsellor, you are likely to have your own therapy rooms. If you are just starting out and wish to specialise in grief counselling, you may not have a professional office yet. It is important to note that grief counselling does not have to be carried out in a professional place of work. You can do house calls or arrange to meet your client at a chosen place. Clients may need counselling at hospital, at home, or prefer to come and see you at your place of work. This should be discussed clearly with the clients and also to look at goals and objectives.

Although counselling can take place anywhere, grief therapy should be set in a professional environment.

Although everyone is entitled to have counselling when dealing with such a loss, it's important to consider who is going to need counselling. If the death has been part of a family tragedy, is sudden and traumatic, then it may be that you must counsel several people of the same family in order to help them through the situation.

This may not be possible of course.

Certainly there is no evidence that all grieving individuals will even benefit from counselling. There is a second train of thought which gives the assumption that some people will need help but it is best to wait until they begin to experience difficulties and to recognise their needs so that they can reach out to you. From a business perspective, this is far more cost-effective but it does mean that potential clients (even those you have been working with) will experience distress before they reached the point where they admit help is required.

One of the main at-risk types when it comes to bereavement will be 'the young woman or man with few relatives close by and who has young children to support.' This type of individual may be shy, introverted and dependent. The death will have caused an increasing amount of stress, the loss of financial income, there may be difficulties with children who in their own way are trying to come to terms with their loss. On the surface, the remaining parent may appear to be coping but inside, there may be feelings of anger, self-reproach or desperation.

Although a great deal of research has gone into grief and bereavement, the difficulties experienced in one research group may be totally different in another. It's always best to take an instinctive response towards counselling once you have listened fully and ascertained the best approach.

Whatever the reasons for the client to seek out help, there are certain principles that should be followed if the sessions are going to be effective.

Firstly, the client has to come to terms with the loss and this is not easy. Even when there is advance warning, a sense of disbelief is likely to be felt. Nothing will seem real. So the very first stage of counselling is to help the client develop awareness about those moments leading up to death and the moment of passing so it becomes real. With this, comes awareness that the individual is not going to return. This may sound brutal but acceptance is vital so that they can deal with the full emotional impact. Avoidance will not help.

One of the best ways to help your clients to face awareness is to talk about it. You can encourage the client to tell you what happened.

For example:

- Where did it happen?
- When did it happen?
- How were they told?
- Where were they when they first heard?
- What was discussed at the funeral?

These questions are centred around the client opening up and discussing the death. Often people have to replay it over in their minds before they can start to realise the enormity of what has happened. In studies, some people have admitted that it is taken up to three months before they could truly start to believe. It helped to visit the grave or where the ashes were scattered, and this eventually helped them to define the truth of their situation.

Another way that you can enable the client to start talking, is to ask them whether they visit the grave and how they feel when there.

Some clients - especially those who favour avoidance, will not visit the grave and so you can take the conversation down the route as to why. Certainly some clients will need to be encouraged to visit and this can form part of their grief work. All of this of course is done with great sensitivity and you need to develop an instinct as to when this suggestion should occur.

Although you can prompt your clients to discuss the situation surrounding the death, the most important aspect once they do is for you to listen and to be patient. Those who have experienced grief, often do not want to talk about it so you may have members of the family all suffering in their own way with one person needing to talk about the situation and others practising avoidance. Family members may not realise the importance of others being able to talk and to discuss their loss. Grief in all its various forms can serve to divide a family.

Often clients will come to see you because they are expecting some sort of miraculous result, they are looking for a quick fix, a quick solution or magic pill that will help them to work through their pain. Helping these types of clients to accept the situation and, to ultimately work through their feeling can be difficult. The strength of their emotions can be extraordinarily intense and can include feelings of anxiety, helplessness, loneliness and anger. There may even be guilt interlaced with these emotions.

As a counsellor you need to be able to identify the emotions experienced so that you can help the client work through them. This is not always easy especially if the client is practising avoidance or is unable to identify how they should feel through the multiple emotions that are fluctuating one after the other.

Anger

We've mentioned that anger is a surprisingly common emotion after someone has died. Anger often comes from frustration and it may be as a result of helplessness. Certainly, when you meet a new client and start to unravel their emotions, you will often find that their anger is very real and although it might not be directed towards the deceased, it is likely to have been directed onto others. This might be someone at the hospital, a doctor or even other member of the family. Of course there can be other issues in place:

- Fear of being alone
- Fear of coping
- Fear of not being loved
- Fear of failing etc.

For those who experience strong anger, do note that it can be turned inwards. It can manifest as feelings of depression, become deeply interlinked with guilt (perhaps relief that the individual died and is not suffering) or there may be confusion – and unexpected emotions. They may lose a little of their own identity or experience doubts about their future or even start to develop lower self-esteem. Decision making might be impossible. They may also be angry at their failure to prevent the death.

This anger is very real even if misplaced.

Unfortunately, anger which is internalised in this way could lead toward suicidal thoughts. It's important to voice your concerns if you think that this is likely and one simple question regarding this can help the client to take less destructive action.

Certainly some of their anger will stem from their situation and unresolved issues but, it may not be just the loss that is creating the problem, rather, it may act as a trigger.

Although in a counselling session an open honest approach is best, if you take the direct approach to discussing the anger, you are probably likely to receive anything but an accurate response. Quite often the client will be lying to themselves and on the surface, believe they are not angry. They'll respond with questions asking how they could be angry with the deceased and will relay many positive attributes about this individual.

Sometimes it takes a different approach to be able to reveal the truth. With this in mind, start to discuss any anxieties that they may feel. This might be in respect of day to day life, work or even family issues. This is often a positive approach to take because they then may open up and state their true situation which can lead to feelings of anger coming out. Sometimes, you have to be a little devious when counselling so to enable the client to respond.

Asking the client if they miss their loved one or what they miss about this person will often be the trigger to bring on genuine feelings of sadness and tears. You can also ask leading questions i.e. what they don't miss about the individual. Too often during grief, we put our loved ones on a pedestal and we remember all that we loved, forgetting the reality of the situation where the person may have been annoying, selfish or uncaring etc., or, they may even have had behavioural or psychological issues. This doesn't make them less of a person but the truth is important. It brings the reality of the situation back.

The most important element of a successful counselling session is for the client to be able to open up and start talking

You may find with some clients that they are only too happy to discuss their negative feelings and in this case, you have to help them bring out their true feelings – there are usually positive thoughts within. The reason for this is that when a client focuses mainly on the negative, it enables them to stop feeling the same level of pain – so yes, it's another avoidance tactic.

The route to recovery is then through the admittance of love, sadness, pining etc. Sometimes grief plays tricks on us and while some clients will display anger or, will remain in a numbed state for longer – you will also have those who will not talk negatively about a loved one (setting them up on a pedestal) or those who will talk about the negatives (and display avoidance tactics).

Guilt

Guilt is quite a common reaction after someone has died. Although we know that death is always a possibility in life, we often do not give it due respect. We focus on living and think that death is always a long way off when in reality, it can hover and take some by surprise. Guilt can occur if a client has been unable to impart their feelings to a loved one and so feels regret and guilt, even experiencing feelings that they may have let them down. While this may be true or not, feelings of guilt must still be dealt with.

Guilt also occurs if an individual feels they did not provide sufficient support or care for their loved one or didn't react in time, these feelings can magnify and intensify, leading them to feel that had they done so, the death may have been prevented. This is particularly true when someone loses a child in that they were unable to prevent the child from being in pain or from dying. They feel that they should have been the one to die and not the child. This type of guilt although irrational, centres completely around the circumstances and of course, the strength of a parent's love.

Within the counselling session, you can help alleviate these feelings by testing the reality of their guilt.

As a prime example, grieving parents might say that they did not do enough for their child. In this case, your leading question is regarding what they did actually do. You can continue to prompt them until they can see the amount that was done. You can even use this technique when discussing the areas in which they believed they failed. Quite often, by talking it through, prompting them and leading them through these dark thoughts, they will realise that they were not responsible.

Of course, sometimes their guilt will be real and more difficult to help resolve. It's then important to make sense of the situation.

Anxiety

We all deal with our emotions in multiples of ways. After anger or guilt, there is often helplessness and frustration. Much of this type of anxiety is created through our belief that we cannot get by on our own. Although this will usually ease as time passes, it is a very real fear. In counselling, you must help the individual to recognise how much they have managed to do, building up their confidence levels. This will grow slowly and surely. Your goal is to put their anxiety and helplessness into perspective. In addition to feeling that they are unable to cope, another anxiety is the awareness of death itself. It is something that we are all aware of throughout our lives that as we are born, at some point we must die.

We are all a little guilty of avoidance and have a natural fear of death. We try not to think about it but when someone close to us dies, it forces us to face acceptance of our mortality. This heightens our awareness and can lead to constant levels of anxiety. This is a genuine fear so guide clients through these feelings carefully.

Sometimes it is better to not address it directly but to monitor and see whether this awareness gradually fades. For other clients, you will sense that it is helpful to discuss it and ask them to talk about their apprehensions. Sometimes bringing it out into the open enables them to unload their concerns and throughout talking, feel a sense of relief.

This really is a matter of judgement.

Sadness and tears

The grief process can leave the client feeling completely bereft of emotion or the opposite - feeling as if they are unable to stop crying. It's important to acknowledge their sadness and to discuss how much they are crying. People often feel guilty about crying but it is alright to encourage it. It is a healthier way of coping.

Often people will try to avoid crying constantly in front of others, they will feel embarrassed by what they see as weakness or, will not wish to add pressure on friendships or loved ones who are also suffering. Alternatively, some people do not like to show their deep emotions and prefer to feel their pain when alone. Counselling can help the individual to see the true reality of any situation, to change their perspective and to understand why they feel a certain way. Crying may be a necessary part of the grieving process for this client. It's important to establish the reason for crying, is it just sadness, or is there another reason underneath that they are not telling you?

Crying alone will not be sufficient to move the grieving process forward. So from a counselling perspective, it's useful to help the client identify the true meaning of their tears and consider the emotion underneath. The sadness must actually mean something. It doesn't matter what the emotion, it needs to be understood before it can be resolved. This is why the counselling process can be quite difficult and it's only through practice and being able to develop a more instinctive approach to your role, connecting to the client and, defining the best route forward, that you will help them to progress. Otherwise, clients can remain stuck in their grief.

Those suffering from bereavement must be able to experience and identify the emotions. They have to feel it, live it and realise that these emotions should be released. Understanding the extent of their pain and acknowledging it is a very healthy approach.

Moving forward

For many individuals, carrying on or coping without their loved one is one of the hardest things they will ever do. Certainly after death, it is common for them to experience a great many obstacles or problems and these can seem insurmountable. In fact, it often highlights that they are truly alone and they feel isolated. When you lose someone to which you were attached, there's no possibility of discussing the situation, of problem-solving, of making light a serious situation. The client often feels totally abandoned and lonely – even if there is a support network around them.

Often in a family unit, there is the primary decision maker. If this person dies, the individual left behind is not able to make decisions on their own, this is particularly frightening for some people. They feel helpless, frustrated by problems and, even start to feel anger at the deceased for leaving them alone. This can happen especially if the client has rushed the grieving process and has practiced avoidance. If this happens, you may need to take them back through the steps.

From a counselling perspective, if you have identified this, your role is to help the individual learn effective coping mechanisms and to strengthen decision-making skills and in this way, they are able to take over the role of primary decision-maker. Although they will still be sad and lonely, the process of managing their own life will help to boost morale, giving them a reason to continue.

When not to make decisions

Generally, anyone who has experienced a loss and who is in the process of grieving, they should be discouraged from making important decisions that will ultimately change their life completely. It's just too soon. This includes selling up the house, changing jobs, or moving away etc. There is often a desire to get away, to leave everything behind and to start life over. But your client's judgement is likely to be impaired at this point. Some people will want to rush through the clearing out stage as if this is going to immediately help them to move on with their lives. There is of course no cheating the grieving process. Those who rush into this act, often regret making such decisions later on.

Another aspect of counselling is to find the meaning of death. For any client who witnessed their loved one drinking themselves to death or, taking drugs, the reason will be plain and clear but understanding why they did so and making sense of it will at least help.

It is when the death cannot be explained that the shock is even greater and harder to come to terms with. If someone has been murdered or killed in a freak accident, it's hard for those left behind to be able to accept such a situation because it doesn't seem real and there's no real reason why this person should have died. Often, to make sense of it, or, to at least take action, people set up memorials or establish a charity in this person's name. It adds a positive element to a bleak situation.

But although finding the true meaning of the loss is important, it also brings up a new challenge as to how the individual left behind has become different because of it. This may be that the grieving person now feels challenged by their situation. They may lose their self-esteem and confidence and feel that they have lost control in life. Again, self-doubts come to the fore or, they also feel shaken as to their own mortality.

Note: Clients will generally move through the grief process at a stage that is right for them.

Some clients will respond more quickly to the sessions and will be more adaptive and accepting, others will take much longer and will find it difficult to move forward or to even except that the situation has happened. Once you are able to help the client progress through the various emotions up to this point, you can then help them to find a new place in their life for the person they have lost.

This may sound strange but it does allow your clients to then move forward and to start forming new relationships.

You will sense when the client is ready for this next step. A great way to do so is to ask them to reminisce - although some of your clients may not need any encouragement for this. Once they have reached the point where they can look back and reflect with a smile, they are ready for the next step – even if it should be tentatively approached.

Some clients will be ready to accept and give love again. But not all your clients will want to do this. They may feel that they will only dishonour the memory of that person. It doesn't matter if it is a partner or a child, they may not wish to embrace this type of attachment again feeling they cannot possibly replace their loved one. Of course this is true, but moving on isn't about replacing anyone, it's about filling a void and, still living. When you broach the subject with some clients, you may see the relief in their eyes that it is ok for them to move on in life and to welcome in new relationships.

Some clients will want to rush this stage. They may be desperately lonely and feel a need to fill this deep void within. Just prompt them to ensure they are doing this for the right reasons. There is little point rushing to make a decision that will affect them for years to come. Finding someone new quickly, can actually prevent the individual from truly mourning and experiencing their loss.

While they might be keen to do just this, it certainly will not help a new relationship as the new individual must feel loved or appreciated for themselves and not just be there as a replacement.

Module Three

Self-Assessment Tasks

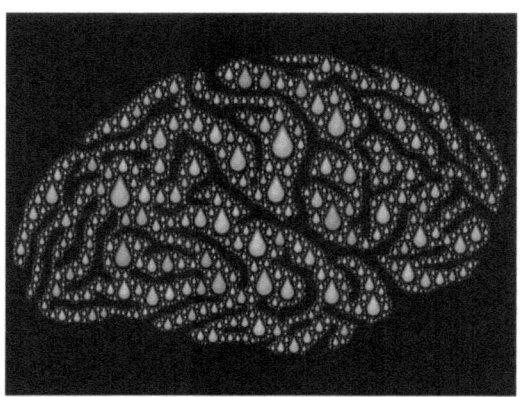

Task:

What are the four stages of goals in grief counselling?

Task:

Consider how you can help a client to reveal their true feelings especially those who may be lying to themselves.

Please note that these self-assessment tasks are to ensure your understanding of the information within each module. As such, do not submit them for review with KEW Training Academy.

Module Four

Grief and the Family

Much of the information that we have covered so far relates to the client's relationship with their loved one. But in the main, these types of significant losses i.e. the husband, the wife, father or mother figure occurs in the context of the family unit. Therefore, when counselling, it's wise to consider the entire family unit and the impact on them.

There are many variables here, a family may have been very close-knit and supported each other totally. Or, the family unit may have been tested to breaking point. Certainly, a family may be divided by the behaviours of an individual within it.

Whatever the environment usually, the loss of a significant family member can certainly unsettle this balance. You must be prepared to take a holistic approach when dealing with the family unit, everyone is different, they all have needs and will be at varying stages of the grieving process.

If you can understand the position held by the deceased within the family, you will have a better idea as to how the other members will be able to adapt to life thereafter. There are many factors that can impact the mourning process and these will be dependent on the roles played by those who are left. You may discover that there is a power shift within the group and younger members of the family are striving for a more dominant role (even if subconsciously), others will play a more communicative role, and you may have someone striving for more affection and reassurance.

Certainly, family dynamics can hinder the whole grieving process.

Let's be clear, a family (dysfunctional or not) works as a unit and each member will have a distinct influence on the other. Therefore what affects one, will affect another. You may find that group family sessions are beneficial but this does depend on the circumstances and the willingness of those involved. It may not be possible to treat each individual personally and to help them deal with their grieving journey certainly without impacting the rest of the family.

Often, tempers fray and formerly solid bonds can begin to fracture-often caused through stress and uncertainty. So, when counselling, consider family grief as a collective as well as individual grief which impacts members of the family separately.

Communication in counselling is always important but you also have to remember that families will vary in their communication skills and may or may not be openly expressive. If this is the case, they may struggle to open up in a counselling session. Those families that are prepared to be open in their discussions about their lost family member tend to cope far more efficiently than those families who are unable to be open with their feelings.

There are lots of factors in play here.

If individuals are not able to be open about their emotions including all that has been mentioned previously i.e. anger, regret etc. their grieving processes will last a lot longer. A key point for looking at a family unit is to help them realise that unresolved grief now will stop the healing process and just as importantly, is going to affect the ability to cope with loss across future generations.

Unresolved issues do not go away, they fester and impact every aspect of life going forward. Where possible, it is useful to be able to reflect over two generations and to understand how they function as a family unit and also to look at individual patterns of behaviour.

The functional position

Take a look at the role which the deceased individual held within the family unit. If one of the parents died, their role would be very important. Whatever their role within the family, the death will undoubtedly disturb the natural balance of the unit. When a family functions well, there is a sense of calm and security within the unit. When there is a loss of a family member, the family may feel deprived and uncertain how to proceed without this individual. After all each person plays a very important role, even the children will have their designated place within the group.

We always tend to think of family units as being close and supportive but this is not always the case. Within your counselling sessions, you may discover that if a child or teenager died, there are feelings of guilt manifesting in one of the siblings. Perhaps there was no love lost between them or they were jealous of each other. The remaining sibling resented the other from having too much attention or for their popularity or even, that their personalities clashed. Siblings do not have to get along but unresolved issues must be corrected after death.

Of course, negative feelings can manifest. The child may start having anger issues or become demanding for attention. They may become socially inept, introverted or even aggressive. They may not wish to talk about their true feelings to their parents but start lashing out in other ways.

If your clients are the younger members of the family or, adolescents, the death of either parent is going to have a detrimental impact on their emotional development. Certainly on an external level, their situation will change dramatically. The death of the family breadwinner is likely to bring a whole set of problems and ones where the adolescents have no idea how to resolve. In addition, their security and safety foundations will be fragmented.

It's important to assess the emotional integration of the family. A well-connected family will be able to help support each other far more than a family that is less integrated. Certainly family members may start to respond with physical or emotional symptoms or, the death creates social misbehaviour. Sometimes this can be avoided through individuals attending the counselling sessions where they can be heard and feel that they are in a safe environment. There is no doubt that expression is a vital part of the grieving process and so encouraging your clients to talk openly and honestly will help them to avoid maintaining a festering wound within.

Some families do not place great emphasis on emotions and so for these families, you may have to work extremely hard building up trust and rapport and giving them the power to voice their concerns. Some people find it very difficult to express their feelings but more than this, to even identify their feelings. This will extend the grieving process.

Note that unresolved issues can lead to unhealthy behaviours and trying to bury the hurt or grief i.e. drinking too much, taking drugs or behaving outrageously is not going to help.

The grieving process for a family unit echoes the tasks outlined in previous models with some adaptations of course. The families must adapt to the death, recognising their loss and believing it to be true. Avoidance issues can easily occur so each member must acknowledge their grief and this a healthy way to cope with it. It also means that the family unit must reassign roles as necessary to avoid any feelings of chaos and restructuring the unit so that there is balance in life once more.

It sounds very straightforward if we talk of communication and family members opening up and talking to each other about their feelings and how it has affected them personally. But not all family units are able to do this but it certainly should be encouraged. By doing so, they will gain a greater insight into the deceased member too because we all have our own perceptions and experiences within our family units and so by sharing these experience, it brings back a sense of unity and understanding for those remaining. Importantly, it adds a richness to the memories of the lost loved one.

Certainly research indicates that those families who cope more efficiently after the death of a family member are those able to tolerate differences between them and the others – and it also improves where there is communication.

Losing a child

When a child dies, the family unit can be impacted greatly and the loss can create complicated grief reactions. Any siblings may feel the weight of expectancy upon them or absorb their fears as a result of the loss. Some parents become stifling to the rest of the family thereafter so freedom may be reduced and children may feel trapped within the confines of the family unit that although caring is claustrophobic. This is an element of counselling that you will need to work on.

Sometimes parents (even unwittingly) place any surviving children into a difficult situation where they become a substitute for the child that was lost to them. They often endow the other children with qualities that belonged to the deceased child. If the parents go on to have more children, it can result in the next child being given the same name or, one that is quite similar. A family with healthy perspectives on life, are usually able to accept the death (eventually) and acknowledge the loss of any child without trying to make the other children fill this void.

Depending on whether the family are openly communicative or not, discussing the situation will help the healing process.

Some families cope by suppressing the facts surrounding the death of their child. On occasion, you may counsel families where children who were born afterwards do not know anything about their dead sibling. The parents may not talk about the deceased child, but there is often an awareness in the other children that something is wrong, that facts are hidden or that some secret is being kept from them. This does not in any way help with the family bonds. In fact, quite often, the parents only reveal the true situation when they themselves are ill or dying. Irrespective of the age of the remaining children, you must advocate the importance of communication.

By behaving in a healthy productive manner at this point, will enable the children to adopt a healthier approach to life and death going forward. Too often, parents try to protect their children from the loss-perceiving it to be far too morbid for young children to cope with. But in fact, children are surprisingly resilient and learn far greater lessons and behaviours in life if they are involved.

When they are shut out of the grieving process, it can lead to their feeling unworthy, unwanted and unloved. Children certainly have a difficult time of it when it comes to telling other people about how they feel. Often they can be encouraged to hide their feelings or to pretend to be happy. Where there are less than adequate communications in the family unit, children will often try to seek out their own answers to questions and this may be far beyond their existing abilities.

Friends and family members may not know how to react to the loss of a child either, they may not even know what to say or do to be supportive. Although a family unit or support network may have good intentions in the first instance, as time progresses there may be an inclination to talk less about the child rather than keeping the memory alive.

There is often a sense of disbelief when a child dies because parents are expected to outlive their children. This alone can lead to a sense of guilt. Also, it depends just how the child has died. A parent may feel that they have been negligent in care and that it was their responsibility look out for them. This may be true. Irrespective, it must still be brought out into the open.

If you have clients where this type of situation is present, tread carefully. Prompt them to open up to you and talk. If you have created a safe environment, they should be able to do so. Support them as they try to make sense of it all in their mind. Remember, it takes time.

There are different types of guilt such as:

- Causal guilt - this is where death occurs as a result of a disorder that has been inherited
- Moral guilt-caused through some moral event in a parent's present or earlier life

- Survival guilt-this occurs if the parent and child were involved in the trauma but the parent survives
- Recovery guilt-this is where the parents will feel guilty as they start to move on with their lives

Although there is always a sense of blame when death has been sudden or dramatic, many parents who lose children feel the need to lash out verbally. Although mothers feel this way, it is often fathers who feel the need to react and seek retribution. This is true even if the child has died of natural causes. The blame, which is still deeply felt, is often then turned toward a family member who takes on the role of scapegoat.

As an example of this, the younger child who died when in the care of the older child.

As a counsellor, you need to be aware of the dynamics of this so as to find the best way for them to resolve their anger issues. When a child dies, both parents will feel the loss deeply but it is true that their experience throughout the grief process will be different. This is understandable when you consider that a mother will have a different relationship to a child than the father. Take into account that they will also have unique coping styles. There is no doubt that these differences constrain the family unit and their relationship. One parent may be more open as regarding emotions and the other may close off their feelings. This can serve to drive them further away from each other.

If you are working with a couple, do make sure that you do not appear to side with the emotionally expressive partner. This can cause the parent who is more introverted to become frustrated with the whole grieving process. At the start of the counselling session, you may find that their communication is centred through you. Certainly, one of the parents may be there reluctantly-often the father. As time progresses, they will realise the benefits of being able to talk and rather than all communications going through you, they will finally start to talk to each other.

You will find that men reveal far less intimate information than women. Indeed, fathers tend to have less social support than women and so they often feel as if they struggle to cope alone. They may also feel that they have to be the strong one in the relationship and support their partner and they do this by withdrawing their own emotions and trying to carry on. This can be seen as being cold and uncaring by the woman.

Note: Although life ticks onwards, there is often guilt if the parents start to be intimate with each other again, they can see this as being wrong to have pleasure and closeness when their child is dead. The opposite can also happen when they need sexual comfort more and more.

You may find during the sessions that there is some discussion of the client having more children. It is worth noting here that parents should not be encouraged to do so at least until they have worked through the trauma of their current loss.

Ultimately there are two main choices for bereaved parents:

1. Learn to live without their child - this requires them to be able to accept, adapt and form new ways of interacting
2. Internalise an inner representation of their child- this enables them to keep their memories close and affords them comfort

You will find that most parents experience disbelief when a child dies. Even though they know that their child has gone, there is another part of them that just does not want to believe it. Some parents hold onto all of the child possessions while others deal with these possessions quickly while they are still in shock. Being practical is a way for them to cope.

For those parents who keep their child's room intact, these are the ones who often struggle with letting go, even years later. As with any type of grief, it's important to find some kind of meaning as to the death. Some parents turn to either religious or philosophical beliefs. Others find peace and comfort through identifying aspects of their child's uniqueness and often set up memorials for the child. Other parents find by becoming involved with others who've gone through similar experiences will give them some meaning in life and it helps them to do this in the name of their child.

Whatever route parents take, it's a very difficult journey.

There are also other aspects to consider within the family unit, such as what happens when the parents die and the children are left behind?

Grieving children

Children who are young or in adolescence, may fail to mourn properly and as time goes by, may experience depression or even find it difficult to form meaningful and close relationships with others. Some research suggests that children will be unable to mourn until their identities are fully formed and this happens at the end of adolescence. Other research indicates that children can begin the mourning process as early as three years of age.

A suitable model of mourning should be found, one that fits the child's unique needs. Perhaps the key component of the mourning process is the emotional reaction to separation. You will see children display grieving behaviours once the figure of attachment has gone, but they may not ,have the cognitive ability to truly understand the meaning of death.

Children who tend to progress through the grieving period more efficiently tend to come from families where there is greater communication about the parent who has died. Active coping methods seem to work better than passive coping methods. Those children who not do so well tend to have experienced many stressors and changes as a result. It may be that their parent was young, or had not coped well. It is very clear that the surviving parent's functioning level is an accurate predictor of the child's ability to adjust and grieve normally.

Typically, the loss of the mother figure is worse for most children than if the father dies. This is because when the mother dies, it immediately instigates many life changes on a daily basis and the mother is usually associated with emotion and nurturing behaviours.

There are three key elements that children need following the death of any parent and these are continuity, nurturing and of course, support. These may not always be forthcoming.

If you are helping children through their grief process, it is far better to have the presence of an adult there who is consistent in the child's life and this will enable the child to feel more confident about expressing their feelings. If you have teenagers and young adults as clients, you will note that they often say they feel differently from their friends – especially if their friends still have both parents and happy home environments. Some teenagers will feel isolated or even older than those in their peer group. There are other issues however and this is dependent on how well the children have adjusted to the loss but even the grieving process which has gone well to a point, can be interrupted when parental dating starts.

Although children may not fully understand the meaning of death, it is true to say that many children will express deep concern for the safety of their one remaining parent even some years after the death of the other parent. They need to know that they will be cared for.

Irrespective of age, those children who are grieving need very clear information about the death. When they are not given any information, their creative minds make up a story and this may be far more frightening than the actual reality. Children need to feel involved and so even though parents will instinctively wish to protect the child, it is worth even discussing the funeral or the memorial service with them. Being open takes some of the fear out of a situation. Of course children are unlikely to have attended a funeral and so would need to be guided as to what is likely to happen.

Remember that children definitely do mourn but it does depend on whether their cognitive and emotional development has progressed otherwise they may not understand what death means. Certainly when losing a parent, although this is a highly traumatic experience, if handled carefully, their development can still continue. The most vulnerable age group in terms of grieving is between the ages of five and seven years. This is because they have developed some cognitive ability but do not have coping capabilities. The mourning process doesn't work in quite the same way either. You will have to modify them taking into account the child's cognitive abilities as well as any social or emotional development.

Module Four

Self-Assessment Tasks

Task:

How would you help parents who are grieving through the loss of a child who died through natural causes?

Task:

How would you help parents who are grieving and now blame each other for the child's death?

Please note that these self-assessment tasks are to ensure your understanding of the information within each module. As such, do not submit them for review with KEW Training Academy.

Module Five

The Counsellor and Grief

We mentioned at the start of this course that offering grief counselling services is not always easy. So let's look at little more closely at how this role can affect you within your daily life. Firstly, when you are working with people who are experiencing the pain of loss, you are probably likely to equate it to losses that you have experienced yourself. While grieving is a natural part of the healing process, it's one thing to teach the mourning process and another thing to be actively living it yourself.

If you have not resolved your own losses adequately, it can lessen your ability to provide helpful counselling to others. If you have gone through all of the grieving stages and have dealt with your own loss, you are more likely to be able to work successfully with your clients. Importantly, you'll have empathy.

As an example: if you have lost your partner either through death or divorce, and it's a recent loss, you may find it incredibly difficult to work with a client whose experiences mirror your own. It will be too painful and too close. If you have worked through your grief and found a way to deal with the loss, then you will be able to help your client. As you can imagine being involved in something that is so painful is likely to impact your ability to be impartial.

Being a counsellor does not give you all of the answers in life.

As much as you help others to cope with their fears and losses, you may have concerns of your own. When you deal with death on a daily basis i.e. you speak to clients who are suffering from varying degrees of grief, it can make the prospect of losing someone you love so much more vivid. Some counsellors find themselves becoming greatly anxious – their fears magnify. They look at ageing parents, the health of their siblings or see their children taking risks and it becomes a huge worry. They can become over anxious and, if this is not dealt with, the anxiety can transform into a relationship that is overprotective and stifling.

When you see a client for the first time, you will be reminded of the inevitability of death and of course, the pain associated with it. It can be worse when the person sitting opposite you is similar in many ways-profession, sex and age and the experience is one you've lived through or are worried about. It can increase your own anxieties. We all have to come to terms with our own mortality but if this is not resolved, it can actually hinder your effectiveness.

Although this course is theoretical, we strongly encourage you to explore your personal history of losses. This will help you to be more effective as a counsellor but it will also help you to understand the whole process of grieving. This may actually help you personally but, it will certainly help you professionally.

Consider any bereavements and how you felt. Then emotionally consider the first stage of grief and explore the whole experience. When you view a section of your own life under a theoretical microscope in this way, it brings home the true reality of life and death. Your own reactions when examining your feelings will highlight the type of coping strategies that you use naturally.

Although exploring your personal emotions may be difficult, it also helps you to make sense of the sort of resources that are available. While everyone deals with the grieving process differently, it does give you a unique insight into the process and enables you to consider what to say to clients.

When you are able to face own life in an honest way and experience those losses, working through them so to resolve them, you may also identify feelings of conflict that has to be identified and ultimately dealt with. It can create surprising revelations into your own personality.

Not everyone can work consistently with people suffering the depths of grief and so there are limitations for many grief counsellors. It may be that you choose to work within general counselling for some of the time and to specialise with certain types of grief counselling at other times, this may limit your involvement with bereavement and enable you to stay focussed, be passionate about your role and to give clients the best support.

Sometimes, you will not be able to help clients. There's no shame in having to refer someone if you cannot help them.

Although your desire may be to help all clients who are undergoing the grieving process, note that it is not essential to do so. Everyone has limitations and it pays to know yours so that you know when to refer client or when to stay the course.

In addition to considering your own associations with death, it's important to avoid stress and burnout and, this means, make sure you do not become overly involved or attached to clients. While you have to care, it's paramount that you retain some professional distance. If a client dies suddenly, you will still need to work your way through the grieving process and to experience the sense of loss. But you will be able to do so in an informed way.

Ultimately, you have a responsibility for your own health and well-being and if you find counselling or specialising in grief therapy too harrowing, you have to accept this and reduce the amount of cases that you are working on or, move into another area of counselling.

If you are able to talk to other counsellors about your own difficult cases, then we recommend that you do so. There has to be an outlet for the feelings that manifest during the sessions. You would not be considering the role of counselling if you did not care about others and it is very easy to take on-board all of the negative feelings and stress as transference is common. If you succumb to stress and it starts to affect your health, you will be no good at helping others so put your own needs first, consider what you want to achieve and how you will achieve it and take advantage of your counselling skills so as to ensure you stay healthy, productive and able.

Module Five

Self-Assessment Test

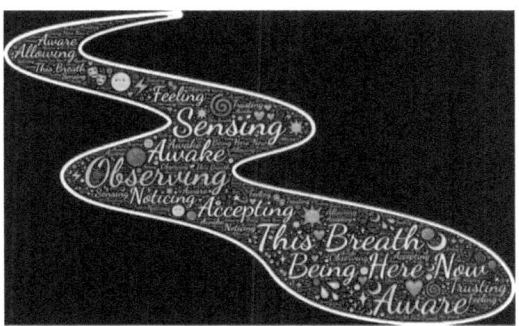

While this course is very much about the understanding of grief and how it affects people in a variety of ways, there has to be an emphasis on the practical elements of helping the bereaved so you feel more confident when you begin. As such, the following tasks in the form of role-play should be practiced with friends or family to help improve your understanding and ability to cope in these situations. You may struggle to know what to say or do initially but with practice, you'll develop an understanding of the necessary steps.

Choose three scenarios as a minimum and write up your experience as if in a case study depicting your experiences, difficulties, errors made or, lessons learned. State clearly which role-play sequence you have used. These role-play examples should be sent with the final test paper for review at the end of this course.

Role-Play 1: Unable to accept the death

A client comes to you after losing their partner in a freak accident. They are unable to accept that their partner is dead. Role-play the situation out considering how you would aid their grieving process using the steps outlined in this course.

Role-Play 2: Anger issues

A client comes to you with obvious anger issues which started after the loss of a sibling. The client acts in a very unkind way about the deceased, how do you help this client through the grief process?

Role-Play 3: Attachment issues

An adolescent seeks out your counselling skills and it becomes clear they have unresolved grief issues due to the loss of a parent several years before. Behaviour (socially) is manifesting and out of control. How do you help this client?

Role-Play 4: Guilt

A woman comes to see you filled with regret and guilt for not believing that her husband felt ill. He died of a heart-attack when out and she cannot move forward with the grieving process until her guilt issues are resolved.

Role-Play 5: Shock and Guilt

A young client comes to see you and it is obvious that this client is in shock. In this case, a freak accident occurred and a close friend was killed outright. Your client survived. Explain how you would help this client.

Role-Play 6: Anxieties

A new client explains that he/she is experiencing regular panic attacks and is panicking about the thought of death after the loss of a parent. How do you help this client?

Role-Play 7: Unable to Cope

A client has spent many years with a partner who has now died. This partner was the decision-maker and now, your client is under a great deal of stress and is terrified of having to cope alone. How can you help the client to feel able to cope as part of the grieving process?

Role-Play 8: The Carer

A client tells you that they are struggling to accept the death of a parent after a long illness. You discover that the client was the parent's full-time carer and now has a large void to fill in life. How can you help this client?

Role-Play 9: Losing a Child

A client is struggling to come to terms with the loss of a child and is not coping at all well even though there are two other children. You notice that the client has started to place character traits from the dead child onto the other children, how can you help this client to resolve this issue and to grieve normally?

Role-Play 10: Acting Irrationally

Your client appears to not be coping with the sudden death of a partner. He/she is also trying to move the grieving process on and has eradicated every item of clothing or items belonging to the partner from the house and is now contemplating selling the house and moving away. What can you do to help this client start the grieving process?

Please take your time with these role-play scenarios. They are very important and can help you to feel much more confident. We suggest practicing them all but only require three completed essays/role-play case studies.

Final Assessment Paper

Congratulations on completing this professional self-study course on Grief and Bereavement Counselling. We hope that you have found it informative and are ready to embark upon your new career. Please take time to complete the Final Assessment Paper in full and then send to: courses@karenewells.co.uk

Following satisfactory review, you will be awarded a professional certificate of merit entitling you to practice.

1. Attach your three role-play style case studies to the email and ensure you have written up your notes in full.

2. What have you most learned through studying this course?

3. Who is George L. Engel?

4. What was John Bowlby's views on feeding and sexual behaviour?

5. Explain avoidance in connection with grief

6. How many phases of mourning are there?

7. List the four **goals** in relation to mourning

8. List the four insecure/attachment styles

9. Is it usually worse for a child to lose the mother or father figure?

10. List the three coping styles

About

The KEW Training Academy was established in 2006 by Karen E. Wells to fill a gap in the market for online courses that make learning fun, educational and easy. The KEW Training Academy offers easy and effective solutions that work for you either personally or professionally. Your course has been tailored from years of experience enabling you to achieve the goals that give you the key to freedom. www.kewtrainingacademy.com

Additional Courses

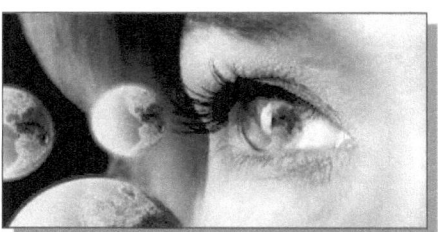

Online Diploma Training Course in Hypnotherapy - Become a Qualified Hypnotherapist

Become a fully qualified Hypnotherapist with this fully accredited Online Training Course in Hypnotherapy. This course gives you all the tools to become a fully recognised and competent Hypnotherapist.

This course is delivered via an E-Learning portal where you work through the course module by module in your own time. It includes a comprehensive training manual, scripts, inductions, and consultation forms for your client, a BONUS Ultimate Relaxation Hypnosis MP3 and unlimited & dedicated support from the tutors via online forums. Everything you need to get you from the sofa at home to being the therapist in your area.

Enrol here

Online Diploma Training Course in Past Life Regression - Become a Qualified Past Life Therapist

The KEW Training Academy is offering this Online Training Course for **Past Life Regression Training** for those with an interest in Past Lives who want to start up or expand their practice by using Regression techniques for this lifetime or for Past Lives. This course is unique and offers training in Past Life Therapy that is not offered elsewhere anywhere!

Enrol here

Online Diploma Training Course - Life Between Lives - Between Lives & Beyond. Become a Qualified LBL Therapist

The KEW Training Academy is offering this Online Training Course - **Life Between Lives – Between Lives & Beyond** for those that have prior experience of Past Life Regression and wish to expand their practice into Life Between Lives Regression.

Life Between Lives was discovered by Dr Michael Newton who was the pioneer for this work. Michael has now retired but has formed TNI (The Newton Institute) based in the US to carry on his legacy.

Enrol here

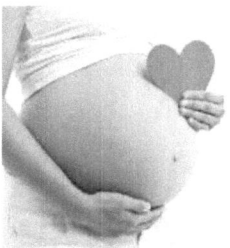

Online Training Course - Easy & Relaxed Childbirth

This Online Training Course is for existing therapists that wish to expand their practice by offering personal & group sessions to pregnant ladies that want to have an Easy & Relaxed Childbirth.

Enrol here

Online Diploma in Mindfulness

Mindfulness is a state of active, open attention on the present moment. When you are Mindful, you can observe your thoughts & feelings with judging them good or bad. Instead of life passing you by, Mindfulness enables you to live in the moment and awaken to each experience of your day and life.

Enrol here

Online Diploma Training Course - Future Life Progression

The KEW Training Academy offers this Online Training Course for Future Life Progression Training for those that have experience in Regression already.

This course is for those who want to expand their practice by using Progression techniques for Future Lives. This course is unique and offers training in Future Lives that is not offered elsewhere anywhere! If you wish to combine Progression with Healing, this is the course for you.

Enrol here

To see all of The Kew Training Academy courses, click here

Credits

All photos are kind courtesy of Pixabay.com

Professional Grief and Bereavement Course

The KEW Training Academy